We Came from Water

*"Reading is not walking on the words;
it's grasping the soul of them."*

— *Paulo Freire*

Other Books by Alan Hill

The Upstairs Country *(Silver Bow 2012)*
The Broken Word *(Silver Bow 2013)*
The Narrow Road to the Far West *(Silver Bow 2018)*

We Came from Water

by
Alan Hill

Silver Bow Publishing
720 – 6th Street, Box # 5
New Westminster, BC
V3C 3C5   CANADA

Title: We Came from Water
Author: Alan Hill
Cover Photo: courtesy of Charlotte Tang-Hill
Cover Design: Candice James
Edit and Layout: Candice James

© 2019 Silver Bow Publishing

ISBN 978-1-77403-091-2 (softcover)
ISBN 978-1-77403-092-9 (e book)
All rights reserved including the right to reproduce or translate this book or any portions thereof, in any form without the permission of the publisher. Except for the use of short passages for review purposes, no part of this book may be reproduced, in part or in whole, or transmitted in any form or by any means, electronically or mechanically, including photocopying, recording, or any information or storage retrieval system without prior permission in writing from the publisher or a licence from the Canadian Copyright Collective Agency (Access Copyright). Copyright to all individual poems remains with the author.

www.silverbowpublishing.com
info@silverbowpublishing.com

Library and Archives Canada Cataloguing in Publication

Title: We came from water / by Alan Hill.
Names: Hill, Alan, 1965- author.
Description: 2nd edition. | Originally published in 2019. | Poems.
Identifiers: Canadiana (print) 20200189840 | Canadiana (ebook) 20200189859 | ISBN 9781774030912
    (softcover) | ISBN 9781774030929 (HTML)
Classification: LCC PS8615.I46 W4 2020 | DDC C811/.6—dc23Silver Bow Publishing

info@silverbowpublishing.com
www.silverbowpublishing.com

Acknowledgments:

I would like to thank the editors of the following journals in which some of these poems have appeared:

Acta Victoriana; Canadian Literature; Dalhousie Review; Event; Grain; Sequestrum; Switchback; Windsor Review; WordWorks

I also would like to thank the following people for their advice and support: Candice James, Jamie Woods, Janet Kvammen, Joanne Arnott, Rachel Rose, Julie MacLellan, and Miranda Pearson

Dedication:

This book is dedicated to Frances, Charlotte and Thomas

We Came from Water

Table of Contents

PART 1: Words for My Father ... 9

Truck Driver... 11
This is the Afterlife ... 12
Nobody Dies in Dreamland ... 13
Let Him Live ... 14
Travel by Train ... 15
Vanilla ... 16
Father, Dying ... 17
Foot Soldiers ... 18
An Introduction to Physics ... 19
Atlantic ... 20
Being God ... 21
Dog Walking ... 22
The Electric Razor ... 23
My Father and His People ... 24
How I Learnt About Concrete ... 25
Where He Lived ... 26
Wearing the Dead ... 27
My Inheritance ... 28
Human Remains ... 29

PART 2: Words for My City ... 31

Mapping the Dominion ... 33
Spider Man on Sixth Street ... 34
The Mirrored Bowl of Midnight ... 35
A History of New Westminster ... 36
Blues for the Penitentiary Dead ... 38
My Winter on Ewen Avenue ... 39
The Royal Columbian... 40
Sandringham Avenue ... 41
An Englishman on 12th Street ... 43
Paul McCartney ... 44
Cary Grant – 525 Sixth Street ... 45

New Westminster - Rock City ... 46
William Blake ... 48
Swimming the Brunette ... 49
A New Westminster ... 50
The Arrival of My People ... 51
The Royal Visit ... 53
Empire Blues ... 54
There Are Good People ... 55
Karl Marx in Starbucks ... 56
The Hermit of Victory Heights ... 57
The River's Reach ... 58
Woodlands Hospital 1963 ... 59
The Commonwealth Blues ... 60
Going Home, Queensborough 1948 ... 61
Beyond Us, the End of the West ... 62
A Hymn for My City ... 64

PART 3: Words for My Wife ... 67

Let us Eat Cake ... 69
Saigon East Vancouver ... 70
Pizza ... 71
Fairy Tale ... 72
Recital ... 73
Heat Wave ... 74
Wedding Night ... 75
Minotaur ... 76
Marriage Guidance ... 77
Fireworks ... 78
Where We Live ... 79

Poet Profile ... 81

We Came from Water

Part One:

Words for My Father

**In Memory of
Michael John Hill**

Aug 8th, 1927 - Feb 15th, 2018

We Came from Water

Truck Driver

Dad is dying, in hospital again,
too weak to stand, to eat, drink.
Death is wringing him out.

Life's fingertips slip one by one from the ledge.
The one with his wedding ring will cling a little longer.

It's also my daughter's tenth birthday party;
an apocalypse of colliding grades of various sugars.

I don't tell her about grandad. Not yet.

No comfortable circle of life,
more a conveyer belt into darkness.
No God anymore to ease the way.

I am surprised how little I feel.
With the very old you get used to last goodbyes.
I have already had a few with dad.

He has given me his facial ticks, moles and marks.
The sly, taciturn, withdrawal of emotion,
sentimentality, free being
that I admire in myself, others.

He won't want flowers;
this man whom I only saw cry once
one summer afternoon
when the cat got crushed by a truck.
The tattooed arm of an unseen driver
lay slumped over an open window.
There was a shake of brakes,
a slow acceleration away.

This is the Afterlife
For my father

You are dying now but we will always have the afterlife.
What I have made for you, that I offer as a gift.

It is here now, if you care to join me.
Open this book, pop it up in folded card,
in the look up from a valley bottom,
into a tangle of car lights through trees on the top road.

One of those cars is you coming home
in the escape from another workday disappointment,
from the office to your consolation; your children.

Of course, we too may have been that disappointment.
Yet, in your diplomacy, you never let us know.
Not then, when we were still young.

Here, in this rest that I offer you,
it is always a November evening just after the rain.
There is a house set back, pasted against open fields;
the garden you made, hidden now until spring.

Then, a drop, a river valley, an alluvial aloneness,
a blackness, tidal in its completeness,
rail lines, the night long shake of unseen freight.

No place is ever really us.
We are awkward, too city, too proud to belong.
This is the nearest we will get: amalgamated, invented
in the outline of mountain tops, the pull of never visited peaks,
stain of crayon, marker in an estuary with an open fist,
offer of bloody palm, unsigned paperwork,
the cracked spine of a discarded book
I never did quite finish
that has its pages laid open to the ocean.

Nobody Dies in Dreamland

As I left for the last time, I hugged my dying father ...

I was amazed. It was my son:
his seven-year old's pulse of hormonal weaponry,
the same conclusive scent of being,
track of curled hair,
spool of roller coaster protein filaments,
split ends that I live to sniff,
plough fingers through.

So it came from this old man
whom I had never hugged before,
would never hug again,
who lived his life, distant as a glint of lesser star,
that could not be seen beyond suburban street glow.

This old man:
who had no God, no heaven, no stone to roll away;

who followed his own obscure footprints
through knee length snow into the silent forest.

So it is with these deceptive beasts:

the old, the brilliantly new
play tricks.

Let Him Live

My father taught me how to knock a nail in,
keep it straight, my fingers intact.

My father taught me how to mix cement,
keep water, powder, in the correct proportion.

My father taught me how to saw wood,
keep the blade free, line intact.

My father taught me how to clip a hedge,
mow a lawn with all my toes still attached.

My father taught me how to change the oil on a car,
check the tires, radiator fluid.

My father taught me how to write a cheque,
open a bank account, hold a pen.

My father taught me how to turn computers on,
play chess, be honest.

My father taught me not to hate,
that there is always good; regardless of race, religion.

My father taught me about music,
that it is good to be alone; That is when you live.

He could not ask me how I felt;
make me know I mattered, that I should be alive.

None of which matters now he is three months dead.
Now, I wish he were here.

Travel by Train

On Sundays,
my father spent an hour in Salzburg, Vienna,
inflated out his cheeks to the beat,
pom pom pomming to Beethoven, Mozart;
the certified, cravat wearing, castle owning classics.

Other times he played in military bands,
strident, to the letter anthems
played by the bored soldiers
of his own youthful conscription.

Dreaming of the pub, girlfriends,
punching the Sergeant Major,
weighing up all this pompous certainty
against their own disinterest.

There was only once his door was shut;
there was no music.

Just his record of old steam trains;
the ones of his childhood,

aging locomotives with broken boilers,
unwashed, straining up obscure inclines.

Old trains a year or two way from the cutters torch,
abandoned to unfashionable freight runs
through unvisited mountains, forest.

The walls would shake, cups rattle,
cats flee as a summit was reached.

the heavy wagons of coal, rock
obstinate, resentful, trying all they could
to pull him backwards into the past.

Vanilla

At the back of the house
the cows in the farmers field had their salt licks.

My family had ice cream.
It went with everything:
crumbles, pies, jellies, laughter, boredom.

With every birthday party that became a food-fight;
with every Christmas that my family never spoke
as we sat like seasick sailors in jauntily angled paper hats ...
miserably watching the Queen's Speech.

What we had was anonymous, uniform,
supermarket own brand.

Always vanilla. Always in those muscle testing plastic tubs:
yolk-yellow, delicious, Eden for the tongue.

My father, the physicist, liked it most.
In its germ-free promise, production-line certainty,
consistent as carpet slippers, ironed pajamas,
the speed of light.,

As certain as the death of God, superstition,
the eradication of war, disease, flared jeans.

In those days labeling wasn't what it came to be.
If you looked closely at the ingredients, it listed them all.
It was a dream you could live with, come to believe:

space exploration, immortal suburbia forever,
a station wagon for everyone,
a job, house, friends for anyone who wanted them,
trampolines, swimming pools, Labradors,
Coca-Cola sprayed like champagne.

Father, Dying

That last summer, father grew strawberries.

Angled his fingers into misty intestines;
curved harvesting knuckles over milk eyed planets,
uncharted Martian moons,
Amazonian boned globes of their bloody red hearts.

In this there was no need for talk,
show feelings, acknowledgment of others

He had been a child of war.
The first thing that he ever did, was learn, not, to cry.

This was him:
alone as he disentangled ripened berries,
birthed them, gave new gravities,
stacked them high,

washed, dressed the bodies of new picked fruit,

prepared them for the dissolve into sugar,
navigation into pies, crumbles,
to become changeling, other
in the oven's heat.

He put jam in jars for the winter months,
passed them onto us for that time
he would no longer have the need to eat.

Foot Soldiers

In the town band
my father grappled with the heart of a drum:

its melodic suicide vest,
a city sized trampoline of near accurate notes
strapped to his chest.

The aged breathed deeply into tubas, French horns
flooded themselves through suburban streets
in a glitter, gush of hair cream;
a tsunami of sock suspenders, string vests.

Once, they had been young:
Had left farms, factories for war.
Had grown up cold, with rickets,
TB, starvation.

Had never been away except to kill;
to be the foot soldiers for someone else's empire.

Once they took a coach trip to the sea ...
this musical militia, thrift store regiment:

farmers, mechanics, drinkers,
hearing aids clipped on like medals.

An Introduction to Physics
1972

Inside, the power plant Christmas party
at my father's work;
young blue-collar guys,
truck drivers, mechanics, warehouse staff
clear the dance floor by just being.

Messengers of messianic blue denim
stand in the certitude of black leather boots
in synchronized, formation, rock n roll,
thumbs fused in their pockets.

They skitter their bodies forward, then back
into stars, squares, new connections,
beginnings.

Outside, the reactor's fat stump,
the bleached skull of itself,
scientific bringer of division,
a bloodless growth on the winter riverbank,
the moan of water
is being pushed through the heart.

Atlantic

In old age, my father struggled
with my insistent interest,
with how I elbowed myself in,
the mere Atlantic unable to stop me,

how I brought my raccoon brained children
that spread themselves as a rash
on his Sudoku-lined, old world hutch.

Last October, I helped him garden
to compensate, once more,
for those years as his hindrance,
expense, worry.

I busied myself, pretended I knew
how to chop wood,
cut grass, dig up dying trees.

I helped him bring up cavities, earth;
unbury roots, free them in death
to the touch of never known air.

We never did talk much.

In the aftermath of our work,
small limbs of the cherry tree
desecrated across the lawn
disappeared.

As evening light peddled itself backward,
branches became obstacles,
barriers to block us from the house;
shield us from the yellow weld
of kitchen window,
the blunt blade of that interior world.

Being God

My father could make anything.
He lived in his workroom,
in his abandoned city:
of dismantled TVs, soft-skulled valves,
boxes of tooth, tough switches,
slit-eyed fuses, their glassy corneas
that refused to blink,
hard mouthed old radios,
scattered shell casings
of broken Bakelite.

He built a greenhouse.
Later, he broke bricks,
hardened concrete into paths,
swapped the engine in my brother's car,
designed storage for my toys, bike.
Later again, in retirement,
he made violins, a cello.

It was his life; persuading things
that they could not exist

unless it was *he* who made them.

Dog Walking

Without your dog, without you,
you, who are two weeks dead,
I stagger down
behind the clump of trees
the red brick, timber cottages
that litter the ridge
smudge themselves
under the sunless, dark green
of late winter.

Down here, where you once walked
the river has risen,
covered my route,
this pathway
that wonders where you are.

The Electric Razor

When dad died
I was left ties, dress pants
with his name sewn in.

Grandad's medals, won
for showing up, standing
at the back.

The electric razor,
sheaved in its immortal blue plastic,
as he had left it the last time.

This man:
who never wore t-shirts,
jeans.

who had one way of being;
formal, decent,
impeccably distant.

whom I had never kissed, held,
told that I love.

Our way; a handshake, smile.

I hugged him once, as he lay
on his hospital bed.

His stiffening grey curls
gave me the scent of my son.

That had to be enough.

My Father and His People

The night of the Queen's Silver Jubilee:
our procession by torchlight, a poor man's Nuremburg,
feudal Disneyland of colliding light, cut price spectacle.

We climbed the mountain track.
Dad, up front, led the pack, this balm of sensible haircuts,
regiment of loyalist drip-dry nylons.

We walked this wire of fire, inch by inch,
up beyond the treeline,
above the valley cut open below us;
illuminated in its obedient streetlight of faded empire,
mathematic shadow of knife edged meadows,
split lung suburbia;
exposed bone of red brick village, terraces,
corner shops laid in hemorrhage by a twisted river.

At the top we found the larger flame,
the bonfire, muscled, uniformed,
the medal of its perfection pinned on the dark,
a forty-foot fist of red, white and blue to colonize
the exile the moon, stars.

There we were:
mouthy, feral. factory boys,
weasel-eyed, obsequious,
loaded on broken pallet, amputated timber,
watched by our wobbly legged old, rich, poor, self appointed,
well-tussled in bunting, embalmed in nostalgia.

Boy Scouts loaded burgers into white-fleshed rolls,
in a heavy artillery of lips, arseholes.

A door of a pit latrine slammed itself shut
in a one-gun salute.

www.ingramcontent.com/pod-product-compliance
Lightning Source LLC
Chambersburg PA
CBHW062147100526
44589CB00014B/1728